BUSSINES STRATEGY FOR BEGINNERS

© **Pd John**

Copyright

All rights reserved, it is not permitted to copy, reprint or duplicate this book without the permission of the author.

Major Prophet PD John
P.O. BOX 4016
Mwanza - Tanzania
Phone number:
+255 762 415 790/ +255 759 204 744
Yohanayona3@gmail.com
www.hl centre.info

ISBN : 9798328830898
First edition ©2024.
Imprint: Independently published

Chief Editor:
Josia pd John
josiajohn735@gmail.com
Dar es salaam - Tanzania
Tel: +255 758588127/ +255 693522834

Dedication:

To all aspiring entrepreneurs, visionary leaders, and the curious minds who dare to dream,

This book is dedicated to you.

May you find within these pages the knowledge and inspiration to embark on your journey into the world of business strategy. Your dedication, passion, and commitment are the driving forces behind innovation and progress. Remember that every great venture began with a vision, and every strategic move started with a single step.

May your endeavors be guided by wisdom, your decisions be fortified by knowledge, and your dreams be realized through diligent strategy.

Here's to your future success in the dynamic world of business.

With the utmost admiration for your determination,

[Prophet PD John]

Acknowledgments:

I am deeply grateful to the countless individuals and resources that have contributed to the creation of this book, *"The Beginner's Guide to Business Strategy."* Writing a comprehensive guide on this topic would not have been possible without their support, knowledge, and encouragement.

I would like to extend my heartfelt gratitude to:

- My family and friends for their unwavering support and understanding throughout this journey.

- My mentors and advisors who shared their invaluable expertise and insights, helping shape the content of this book.

- The dedicated professionals in the field of business strategy who have conducted extensive research and provided the foundation upon which this book is built.

- The reviewers and beta readers who offered constructive feedback, ensuring the clarity and relevance of the material.

- The team at [Your Publishing Company], whose dedication and hard work brought this book to life.

- And, most importantly, to the readers, for choosing to explore the world of business strategy through these pages. Your curiosity and willingness to learn inspire the creation of knowledge.

This book is the result of a collaborative effort, and I am profoundly thankful to each and every person who played a role in its development.

With deep appreciation,

[Prophet PD John]

My Testimony

Personal Testimony: The Birth of a Business Strategy Journey

My journey into the world of entrepreneurship was far from a smooth sail. It was a path filled with challenges, uncertainties, and a burning desire to make a mark in the business world. Little did I know that these struggles would give birth to a work of art—a comprehensive guide on business strategy.

I began my entrepreneurial journey with a dream, a vision of creating a business that would not only thrive but also make a positive impact. Like many aspiring entrepreneurs, I was driven by passion, armed with ambition, and fueled by a deep desire for independence.

However, reality hit me hard. I encountered numerous roadblocks along the way. From financial *constraints that felt insurmountable to facing competition that seemed overwhelming, each challenge tested my resolve.*

One of the most significant hurdles was understanding the intricate world of business strategy. I realized that having a brilliant business idea was not enough. It needed a strategic foundation to transform it into a successful venture. I embarked on a quest to learn, grow, and adapt. I read books, attended seminars, and sought mentorship.

My struggles in understanding and implementing effective business strategies became the driving force behind this work of art. I realized that if I faced these challenges, there were countless others who did too. This realization ignited a passion to compile my knowledge and experiences into a comprehensive guide that could serve as a beacon for fellow entrepreneurs, a roadmap through the complexities of business strategy.

I poured my heart and soul into creating a resource that would simplify the strategic planning process, demystify complex concepts, and provide practical tools and templates. The struggles I faced gave me the empathy to explain these concepts in a relatable way, as if I were guiding a friend through the process.

The personal testimony of my entrepreneurial journey serves as the foundation of this work. It's a reminder that challenges are opportunities in disguise, that struggles can lead to growth, and that every setback is a stepping stone toward success.

I hope that by sharing my story and the knowledge I've gathered, I can inspire and empower others who are on their entrepreneurial journey. May this work be a testament to the belief that with determination, resilience, and the right strategy, anyone can turn their business dreams into reality.

As I reflect on the struggles that birthed this work of art within me, I am reminded of the biblical principle in **Romans 8:28 (NIV): "And we know that in all**

things God works for the good of those who love him, who have been called according to his purpose." *Indeed, my journey was purposeful, and I hope this guide serves as a valuable resource for all who seek to navigate the world of business strategy.*

Preface:

Welcome to ***"The Beginner's Guide to Business Strategy."*** This book is your gateway to the dynamic and exciting world of business strategy—a world where innovation, planning, and execution intersect to shape the destinies of companies, both large and small.

In today's rapidly evolving business landscape, understanding and implementing effective strategies are crucial for success. Whether you are an aspiring entrepreneur, a manager looking to sharpen your skills, or simply someone intrigued by the art of strategic thinking, this book is designed to provide you with a solid foundation in business strategy.

Through these pages, we will embark on a journey that explores the fundamentals of business strategy, from its historical roots to its contemporary applications. You will discover the various types of business strategies, learn how to conduct SWOT analyses, delve into the intricacies of market research, and uncover the secrets of successful competitive analysis. Moreover, you'll gain insights into setting goals, strategic planning, execution, risk management, and so much more.

Throughout this book, you'll find real-world examples, case studies, and practical exercises that will help you bridge the gap between theory and application. Whether you aspire to launch your own startup, lead a team, or contribute to your organization's strategic decisions, the knowledge and skills acquired here will prove invaluable.

The business world is ever-changing, and adaptability is key to thriving in it. Therefore, this book also delves into topics like innovation, sustainability, international strategies, and preparing for the future.

As you immerse yourself in these chapters, remember that the journey to becoming proficient in business strategy is ongoing. Embrace the challenges, embrace change, and embrace the opportunities that lie ahead.

By the end of this journey, you will possess a toolkit of strategic thinking and decision-making skills that can empower you to navigate the complexities of the business world with confidence and purpose.

I invite you to explore the pages ahead with an open mind and a thirst for knowledge. The world of business strategy is at your fingertips, and it's ready to be conquered.

Let's begin.

[Prophet PD John]

Table of Contents:

Copyright I

Dedication: II

Acknowledgments: III

My Testimony V

Preface: IX

Table of Contents: XII

Introduction: XVII

Chapter 1: Understanding Business Strategy 1

   1.1 Defining Business Strategy 1

   1.2 The Role of Strategy in Business Success. 2

   1.3 Historical Overview of Business Strategy ... 3

Chapter 2: Types of Business Strategies 5

   2.1 Differentiation Strategy 5

   2.2 Cost Leadership Strategy 6

   2.3 Focus Strategy 7

2.4 Hybrid Strategies 8

Chapter 3: SWOT Analysis 10

3.1 What is SWOT Analysis? 10

3.2 Conducting a SWOT Analysis 11

3.3 Using SWOT to Develop Strategy 12

Chapter 4: Market Research and Analysis 14

4.1 The Importance of Market Research 14

4.2 Conducting Market Research 15

4.3 Analyzing Market Trends 16

4.4 Identifying Target Markets 17

Chapter 5: Competitive Analysis 19

5.1 Understanding Competitive Forces 19

5.2 Competitive Advantage 20

5.3 Tools for Competitive Analysis 21

Chapter 6: Creating a Business Model 23

6.1 What is a Business Model? 23

6.2 Components of a Business Model 24

6.3 Examples of Successful Business Models 25

Chapter 7: Setting Business Goals and Objectives 27

7.1 SMART Goals 27

7.2 Long-term vs. Short-term Objectives 28

7.3 Aligning Goals with Strategy 29

Chapter 8: Strategic Planning 31

8.1 The Strategic Planning Process 31

8.2 Developing a Strategic Plan 32

8.3 Involving Stakeholders 34

Chapter 9: Implementation and Execution 36

9.1 Turning Strategy into Action 36

9.2 Assigning Responsibilities 37

9.3 Monitoring Progress 38

Chapter 10: Measuring and Evaluating Strategy 42

10.1 Key Performance Indicators (KPIs) 42

10.2 Balanced Scorecard 43

10.3 Adjusting Strategy Based on Results 44

Chapter 11: Innovation and Adaptation 46

    11.1 The Role of Innovation in Strategy 46

    11.2 Adapting to Changing Markets 47

    11.3 Case Studies of Adaptive Companies 48

Chapter 12: Managing Risk in Strategy 50

    12.1 Identifying Business Risks 50

    12.2 Risk Mitigation Strategies 51

    12.3 Crisis Management 52

Chapter 13: International Business Strategy ... 54

    13.1 Expanding Globally 54

    13.2 Cultural Considerations 55

    13.3 International Market Entry Strategies 56

Chapter 14: Sustainable Business Strategies .. 58

    14.1 Sustainability in Business 58

    14.2 Environmental and Social Responsibility 59

    14.3 The Triple Bottom Line 60

Chapter 15: Case Studies 62

15.1 Real-world Examples of Successful Business Strategies 62

15.2 Lessons Learned 63

Chapter 16: The Future of Business Strategy .. 65

16.1 Emerging Trends and Technologies 65

16.2 Preparing for the Future 66

Conclusion: 69

Recap of Key Concepts 69

Encouragement to Apply What You've Learned 71

Appendices: 74

Introduction:

In the grand tapestry of human history, the art of strategy has played an integral role in guiding nations, armies, and individuals toward their desired outcomes. In much the same way, the world of business is a theater of strategy, where decisions made today can shape the destiny of companies for years to come.

In the biblical book of Proverbs, King Solomon, known for his wisdom, wrote: *"The plans of the diligent lead to profit as surely as haste leads to poverty."* **(Proverbs 21:5, NIV)** These words of ancient wisdom highlight the timeless importance of planning and strategy in the pursuit of success. In the realm of business, diligence in crafting and executing a well-thought-out strategy can lead to prosperity, while hasty decisions can lead to financial ruin.

Consider the story of Joseph, as recounted in the book of Genesis. Joseph's ability to interpret Pharaoh's dreams and devise a strategy to store grain during times of plenty saved Egypt from famine. His strategic foresight not only ensured the survival of a nation but also elevated him to a position of authority and influence. This biblical narrative underscores the impact of strategic thinking and planning on both individual and organizational success.

Target Audience and Learning Objectives

This book, *"The Beginner's Guide to Business Strategy,"* is tailored to a diverse audience of individuals who seek to harness the power of strategic thinking in the realm of business. Whether you are an aspiring entrepreneur, a manager aiming to refine your strategic skills, or simply someone curious about the inner workings of successful businesses, this guide is designed with you in mind.

Learning Objectives:

1. **Understand the Essence of Strategy:** Explore the foundational concepts of business strategy, from its historical roots to its modern-day significance.

2. **Master Strategic Thinking:** Learn how to think strategically by dissecting real-world examples and biblical principles to make sound decisions in business.

3. **Navigate Competitive Landscapes:** Gain insights into competitive analysis and discover how businesses can leverage their strengths while mitigating weaknesses.

4. **Plan for Success:** Develop the skills to set meaningful goals, create strategic plans, and execute them effectively.

5. **Adapt and Innovate:** Embrace change and discover the importance of innovation in sustaining business success.

6. **Manage Risk with Wisdom:** Learn to identify, assess, and manage risks through practical strategies, as exemplified by biblical wisdom.

7. **Expand Your Horizons:** Explore international business strategies and ethical considerations in the global marketplace.

8. **Prepare for the Future:** Consider emerging trends and technologies that will shape the future of business strategy.

Throughout this journey, we will draw inspiration from both the wisdom found in the Bible and the practical wisdom of contemporary business leaders. Together, we will uncover the timeless principles and modern applications of strategic thinking, empowering you to navigate the intricate world of business strategy with purpose and wisdom.

Chapter 1:

Understanding Business Strategy

In this chapter, we will delve into the fundamental concepts of business strategy, exploring its definition, its crucial role in achieving business success, and tracing its historical evolution through time.

1.1 Defining Business Strategy

Business strategy is the compass that guides an organization toward its goals. It's the art and science of making decisions that position a company for long-term success. As the Bible wisely states in **Proverbs 16:3 (NIV):** "Commit to the Lord whatever you do, and he will establish your plans."

This verse reminds us that even in the realm of business, careful planning and strategy are vital.

1.2 The Role of Strategy in Business Success

Consider the parable of the wise and foolish builders from the book of Matthew *(Matthew 7:24-27, NIV)*. The wise builder's house stands firm because it was built on a solid foundation, while the foolish builder's house collapses due to a weak foundation. Similarly, in business, a well-crafted strategy provides the foundation upon which a company can weather storms and thrive.

We will explore how a sound business strategy can:

- Provide a clear direction for the organization.

- Enhance decision-making by aligning actions with long-term objectives.

- Allocate resources effectively, optimizing both time and capital.

- Adapt to changing market conditions and uncertainties.

1.3 Historical Overview of Business Strategy

To understand where we are today, we must trace the roots of business strategy. From the military strategies of ancient empires to the modern corporate boardrooms, strategic thinking has evolved significantly.

We'll journey through key milestones in the history of business strategy, such as:

- Sun Tzu's "The Art of War" and its enduring influence on strategy.

- The industrial revolution and the birth of modern business strategy.

- The emergence of management gurus like Peter Drucker and Michael Porter.

- Contemporary approaches to strategy in the digital age.

By exploring these historical perspectives, we gain a deeper appreciation for the evolution of strategic thought and how it continues to shape the business landscape today.

As we embark on this chapter, remember that understanding the essence of business strategy is the first step towards harnessing its power. Just as a ship requires a captain to navigate the seas, a business needs a well-defined strategy to chart its course through the ever-changing tides of commerce.

Chapter 2:

Types of Business Strategies

In this chapter, we will explore the various types of business strategies that organizations can adopt to achieve their objectives. Each strategy comes with its own set of advantages and challenges, and understanding them is essential for effective decision-making.

2.1 Differentiation Strategy

A differentiation strategy is like a beacon that sets a company apart in a crowded marketplace. This strategy involves offering unique products or services that are distinct from those of competitors. Just as the Bible encourages us to be *"salt and light"* *(Matthew 5:13-16, NIV),* businesses employing differentiation aim to shine brightly in the eyes of consumers.

We'll delve into:

- Creating a unique value proposition.

- Building brand identity and loyalty.

- Examples of companies successfully employing differentiation.

2.2 Cost Leadership Strategy

"Count the cost" **(Luke 14:28, NIV)** is a biblical principle that underscores the importance of careful planning. In business, a cost leadership strategy involves becoming the lowest-cost producer in an industry, offering products or services at competitive prices while maintaining profitability.

Topics covered will include:

- Strategies to reduce costs.

- Economies of scale and scope.

- The balance between cost-cutting and quality.

2.3 Focus Strategy

In *Matthew 6:24 (NIV), it is said, "No one can serve two masters."* Similarly, in business, focusing on a specific market segment or niche can lead to success. A focus strategy concentrates efforts on a narrow target market, aiming to meet its unique needs exceptionally well.

We'll discuss:

- Identifying and selecting target markets.

- Tailoring products or services to meet specific customer demands.

- How focus can lead to competitive advantage.

2.4 Hybrid Strategies

Just as the Bible encourages believers to be *"wise as serpents and harmless as doves"* **(Matthew 10:16, NIV),** businesses can employ hybrid strategies that combine elements of differentiation, cost leadership, and focus to adapt to complex market conditions.

We'll explore:

- The advantages of hybrid strategies.

- Real-world examples of companies successfully using hybrid approaches.

- The challenges and trade-offs involved in implementing hybrid strategies.

By the end of this chapter, you will have a comprehensive understanding of the major types of business strategies and how they can be applied to achieve specific business objectives. Remember, choosing the right strategy is like selecting the right tool for a task—each has its purpose, and the decision should align with the organization's goals and market dynamics.

Chapter 3:

SWOT Analysis

In this chapter, we will delve into the powerful tool known as SWOT analysis, which provides valuable insights for strategic decision-making by examining an organization's internal strengths and weaknesses, as well as external opportunities and threats.

3.1 What is SWOT Analysis?

SWOT analysis is akin to self-reflection, a process that allows businesses to take a closer look at themselves and their environment. SWOT stands for:

- **Strengths:** Internal attributes that give an organization an advantage.

- **Weaknesses:** Internal attributes that can be a hindrance.

- **Opportunities:** External factors that present favorable circumstances.

- **Threats:** External factors that pose challenges and risks.

Much like the wisdom in **Proverbs 14:15 (NIV)** that encourages discernment, SWOT analysis equips businesses with the discerning ability to make informed decisions.

3.2 Conducting a SWOT Analysis

Performing a SWOT analysis requires a structured approach. We'll delve into the steps involved in conducting a thorough analysis:

- **Gathering Data:** Collecting information on internal factors (strengths and weaknesses) and external factors (opportunities and threats).

- **SWOT Matrix:** Creating a visual representation of the analysis to identify key factors.

- **Prioritization:** Assigning weight to each factor to determine its relative importance.

- **SWOT Summary:** Summarizing the analysis to reveal insights and patterns.

We'll also discuss the importance of objectivity and involving key stakeholders in the process.

3.3 Using SWOT to Develop Strategy

A well-conducted SWOT analysis serves as a strategic compass, guiding organizations toward informed decision-making. We'll explore how to translate the insights gained from a SWOT analysis into actionable strategies:

- **Leveraging Strengths:** How to capitalize on internal strengths to gain a competitive edge.

- **Mitigating Weaknesses:** Strategies for addressing and improving internal weaknesses.

- **Seizing Opportunities:** Identifying and exploiting external opportunities for growth.

- **Mitigating Threats:** Strategies to navigate external threats and minimize risks.

Real-world case studies will illustrate how organizations have effectively used SWOT analysis as a foundation for strategic planning and execution.

By the end of this chapter, you will have a comprehensive understanding of SWOT analysis as a valuable tool in the strategic toolkit. Like the wisdom imparted in *Proverbs 24:6 (NIV),* "For waging war, you need guidance," SWOT analysis provides the guidance necessary to make informed strategic decisions, positioning your business for success in a competitive landscape.

Chapter 4:

Market Research and Analysis

In this chapter, we will explore the critical aspects of market research and analysis, a cornerstone of effective business strategy. Understanding your market and its dynamics is essential for making informed decisions and achieving sustainable success.

4.1 The Importance of Market Research

Market research is akin to the biblical principle of *"seek and you shall find"* **(Matthew 7:7, NIV).** It involves systematically gathering, analyzing, and interpreting information about a target market, enabling businesses to make data-driven decisions.

We'll discuss:

- **Why Market Research Matters:** Exploring the benefits of understanding customer needs, preferences, and behaviors.

- **Minimizing Risk:** How market research helps mitigate potential pitfalls by uncovering market challenges.

- **Market Research Ethics:** The importance of conducting research with integrity and respect for privacy.

4.2 Conducting Market Research

Effective market research involves a well-defined process. We'll delve into the steps required to conduct comprehensive market research:

- **Defining Research Objectives:** Clarifying what you aim to achieve with your research.

- **Data Collection Methods:** Exploring various research techniques, including surveys, interviews, focus groups, and data analysis.

- **Data Analysis and Interpretation:** Turning raw data into actionable insights.

- **Market Research Tools:** An overview of tools and technologies that aid in data collection and analysis.

4.3 Analyzing Market Trends

Much like the *"signs of the times"* **(Matthew 16:3, NIV)** were to be observed in biblical times, in business, recognizing and adapting to market trends are key to staying relevant. We will explore:

- **Spotting Market Trends:** How to identify emerging trends that could impact your business.

- **Competitive Analysis:** Understanding what competitors are doing and how it affects your market position.

- **SWOT in Market Analysis:** Applying SWOT analysis to evaluate your market position.

4.4 Identifying Target Markets

Just as the Good Shepherd sought the lost sheep *(Luke 15:4, NIV),* businesses must identify and reach their ideal customers. We'll discuss:

- **Segmentation:** How to divide your market into distinct groups based on characteristics.

- **Targeting:** Selecting specific market segments to focus your marketing efforts.

- **Positioning:** Crafting your brand and offerings to appeal to your chosen target markets.

By the end of this chapter, you will recognize the pivotal role that market research and analysis play in developing a successful business strategy. Armed with insights into customer needs, market trends, and competitive landscapes, you'll be better equipped to make informed decisions and effectively position your business in the marketplace.

Chapter 5:

Competitive Analysis

In this chapter, we will delve into the realm of competitive analysis, where we explore the forces that shape the business landscape, the pursuit of competitive advantage, and the tools that aid in assessing and strategizing in a competitive environment.

5.1 Understanding Competitive Forces

The business world is akin to the battlefield, and understanding the competitive forces at play is crucial. We will delve into the concept of competitive forces as elucidated by Michael Porter, and how they impact an organization's strategy:

- **Threat of New Entrants:** Analyzing the barriers to entry in an industry.

- **Bargaining Power of Suppliers and Buyers:** Evaluating the influence suppliers and buyers wield.

- **Threat of Substitutes:** Identifying alternative products or services that could replace yours.

- **Rivalry Among Competitors:** Assessing the intensity of competition within the industry.

- **Complementary Products and Services:** Understanding the role of complementary offerings.

5.2 Competitive Advantage

In business, as in life, having an advantage is often the key to success. We'll explore the notion of competitive advantage—the unique strengths that enable a company to outperform its rivals:

- **Cost Advantage:** Achieving lower production costs than competitors.

- **Differentiation Advantage:** Standing out by offering unique features or value.

- **Focus Advantage:** Concentrating efforts on a specific market segment.

Just as in **Proverbs 22:29 (NIV)** where it says, *"Do you see someone skilled in their work? They will serve before kings,"* competitive advantage elevates a company's standing and influence in the market.

5.3 Tools for Competitive Analysis

To navigate the complex web of competitive forces, businesses employ various tools and frameworks. We will explore some of the most commonly used tools:

- **SWOT Analysis in Competitive Context:** Applying SWOT analysis to understand your competitive position.

- **Porter's Five Forces Analysis:** A deeper dive into Michael Porter's framework.

- **Competitor Analysis:** Strategies for researching and assessing your competitors.

- **Benchmarking:** Comparing your performance against industry standards or competitors.

These tools empower businesses to make informed decisions, adapt to changing competitive landscapes, and formulate strategies that capitalize on strengths and mitigate weaknesses.

By the end of this chapter, you will have gained a deep understanding of the competitive forces shaping the business world. Armed with knowledge about competitive advantage and analytical tools, you'll be well-prepared to assess your competitive position and formulate strategies to excel in your industry.

Chapter 6:

Creating a Business Model

In this chapter, we will explore the concept of a business model, dissecting its components, and drawing inspiration from real-world examples of successful business models.

6.1 What is a Business Model?

A business model is the blueprint that outlines how an organization creates, delivers, and captures value. It's akin to the architectural plans of a building, detailing the essential elements that make a business viable. In the context of business, **Proverbs 19:21 (NIV)** *resonates:* "*Many are the plans in a person's heart, but it is the Lord's purpose that prevails.*" Business models are those purposeful plans to bring value to the world.

6.2 Components of a Business Model

A robust business model comprises several interconnected components, each playing a pivotal role in the organization's success. We will explore these key elements:

- **Value Proposition:** Defining what your business offers and why it's valuable to customers.

- **Customer Segments:** Identifying the specific groups of customers your business targets.

- **Channels:** Outlining how you reach and interact with your customers.

- **Customer Relationships:** Describing how you build and maintain relationships with customers.

- **Revenue Streams:** Detailing how your business generates income.

- **Key Resources:** Identifying the critical assets and resources your business needs.

- **Key Activities:** Defining the essential tasks your business must perform.

- **Key Partnerships:** Exploring collaborations and partnerships that enhance your business.

- **Cost Structure:** Outlining the expenses incurred to operate your business.

We'll discuss how each of these components interacts to create a cohesive and profitable business model.

6.3 Examples of Successful Business Models

Drawing inspiration from real-world success stories can illuminate the possibilities within the realm of business models. We'll explore case studies of companies that have innovatively crafted their business models:

- **Amazon:** A prime example of an online marketplace and logistics giant.

- **Netflix:** A pioneer in the subscription-based streaming model.

- **Uber:** A disruptor in the sharing economy with a unique platform-based model.

- **Tesla:** An innovator in electric vehicles with an integrated energy ecosystem.

These examples will showcase the diversity of business models and the potential for creativity and innovation in shaping successful enterprises.

By the end of this chapter, you will have a comprehensive understanding of what a business model entails, its core components, and how successful businesses have harnessed the power of strategic business modeling to thrive in today's dynamic marketplace.

Chapter 7:

Setting Business Goals and Objectives

In this chapter, we will delve into the art and science of setting business goals and objectives, exploring the SMART framework, the distinction between long-term and short-term objectives, and the crucial alignment of goals with strategic vision.

7.1 SMART Goals

Setting goals is akin to charting a course, and the SMART framework provides a compass for effective goal setting. SMART stands for:

- **Specific:** Goals should be clear, well-defined, and specific in what they aim to achieve.

- **Measurable:** Goals should include criteria for measurement, allowing you to track progress.

- **Achievable:** Goals should be realistic and attainable with the available resources.

- **Relevant:** Goals should align with the broader mission and strategy of the organization.

- **Time-bound:** Goals should have a clear timeline or deadline for completion.

We'll explore how SMART goals serve as a roadmap for businesses, providing clarity and direction.

7.2 Long-term vs. Short-term Objectives

Much like the biblical principle in *Ecclesiastes 3:1 (NIV)* that there is *"a time for everything,"* in business, there is a time for both long-term and short-term objectives. We'll discuss:

- **Long-term Objectives:** These are strategic goals that set the direction for the organization over an extended period, often several years. They define the vision and desired outcomes.

- **Short-term Objectives:** These are tactical goals that help accomplish specific tasks and milestones within a shorter timeframe, usually within a year or less.

Understanding when to focus on long-term vision and when to tackle immediate tasks is crucial for effective goal setting.

7.3 Aligning Goals with Strategy

In *Proverbs 16:9 (NIV),* it is written, *"In their hearts humans plan their course, but the Lord establishes their steps."* Similarly, businesses plan their course through strategic goals, but those goals must align with the broader strategic vision to be successful.

We'll explore:

- **Strategic Alignment:** How to ensure that each goal contributes to the realization of the overall strategy.

- **Cascade Effect:** The process of aligning individual and departmental goals with the organizational strategy.

- **Monitoring Progress:** Strategies for tracking progress toward goal achievement and making adjustments as needed.

By the end of this chapter, you will have the tools and knowledge to set meaningful and effective goals for your business. Just as a ship's crew relies on a well-plotted course to reach their destination, businesses rely on well-defined goals to navigate toward their strategic vision successfully.

Chapter 8:

Strategic Planning

In this chapter, we will dive into the strategic planning process, exploring its steps, the creation of a strategic plan, and the importance of involving stakeholders in shaping the future of an organization.

8.1 The Strategic Planning Process

Strategic planning is akin to charting a voyage; it involves defining where an organization wants to go and how it intends to get there. We'll break down the strategic planning process into a series of steps:

- **Step 1: Establish the Mission and Vision:** Clarifying the organization's purpose (mission) and its desired future state (vision).

- **Step 2: Assess the Current Situation:** Conducting a thorough analysis of internal strengths and weaknesses, as well as external opportunities and threats (SWOT analysis).

- **Step 3: Set Strategic Goals:** Using the SMART framework to define clear and measurable goals.

- **Step 4: Develop Strategies:** Crafting strategies to achieve the defined goals.

- **Step 5: Create an Action Plan:** Outlining the specific actions, resources, and timelines needed for implementation.

- **Step 6: Monitor and Adapt:** Continuously tracking progress, evaluating outcomes, and adjusting strategies as needed.

8.2 Developing a Strategic Plan

A strategic plan is the blueprint that outlines how an organization will execute its strategy. We'll explore the essential elements of a strategic plan:

- **Executive Summary:** A concise overview of the plan's key points.

- **Mission and Vision Statements:** Reiterating the organization's purpose and future direction.

- **Goals and Objectives:** Clearly defining what the organization aims to achieve.

- **Strategies and Action Plans:** Detailing how each goal will be accomplished.

- **Resource Allocation:** Identifying the resources required for implementation.

- **Performance Metrics:** Establishing KPIs to track progress.

- **Risk Assessment:** Evaluating potential risks and mitigation strategies.

We'll also discuss the importance of communicating the plan effectively throughout the organization.

8.3 Involving Stakeholders

Just as in **Proverbs 15:22 (NIV)** where it says, *"Plans fail for lack of counsel, but with many advisers, they succeed,"* involving stakeholders in the strategic planning process is crucial. We'll explore:

- **Who Are Stakeholders:** Identifying internal and external stakeholders with a vested interest in the organization's success.

- **The Benefits of Involvement:** How diverse perspectives can lead to better decision-making and buy-in.

- **Engagement Strategies:** Techniques for engaging stakeholders in the planning process, such as surveys, workshops, and focus groups.

By the end of this chapter, you will have a comprehensive understanding of the strategic planning process and how to develop a strategic plan that guides your organization toward its goals. Engaging stakeholders in this process ensures that the plan is not only well-informed but also well-supported throughout the organization.

Chapter 9:

Implementation and Execution

In this chapter, we'll explore the vital phase of turning strategy into action—implementation and execution. We'll cover the practical steps to bring your strategic plan to life, including assigning responsibilities, monitoring progress, and end with a personal testimony illustrating the importance of effective execution.

9.1 Turning Strategy into Action

A well-crafted strategy is like a treasure map, but it's only valuable if you can follow it to the treasure. We'll delve into the critical aspects of translating your strategy into actionable steps:

- **Execution Planning:** Developing detailed plans and workflows.

- **Resource Allocation:** Assigning the necessary resources, such as personnel, time, and budget.

- **Communication:** Ensuring that everyone in the organization understands their role and the strategic objectives.

9.2 Assigning Responsibilities

Just as a successful military operation relies on a well-defined chain of command, implementing a strategic plan requires clear assignments of responsibility. We'll discuss:

- **Role Definition:** Specifying who is responsible for each aspect of the plan.

- **Accountability:** Creating a culture of accountability where individuals are responsible for their designated tasks.

- **Leadership:** The role of leadership in guiding and supporting the execution process.

9.3 Monitoring Progress

In business, as in the biblical principle of stewardship, we must ensure that resources are used wisely and effectively *(1 Corinthians 4:2, NIV).* Monitoring progress is vital to ensure that resources are directed toward achieving strategic goals. We'll explore:

- **Key Performance Indicators (KPIs):** Defining metrics to measure progress.

- **Regular Review:** The importance of scheduled check-ins and reviews.

- **Adjustment and Adaptation:** Being willing to make changes based on real-time data and feedback.

Personal Testimony:

Throughout this chapter, we've emphasized the importance of effective implementation and execution. Allow me to share a personal testimony that underscores the significance of this phase.

One of the companies I work with faced a significant challenge in executing their strategic plan. They had a great plan in place, but the team struggled with putting it into action.

The company had a huge product launch planned but was struggling to get their sales team aligned with the new direction. The challenges included failure to communicate the new strategy effectively, and lack of training for the sales team on the new product line and sales process.

Initially, the team was getting demoralized due to the delays and lack of success. However, the company did not give up. They invested time and resources in training the sales team, revising their communication plan, and improving collaboration across departments.

As a result of these actions, the product launch was eventually successful, and sales increased significantly. The company's return on investment was phenomenal, thanks to the efforts that they put into executing the strategic plan.

In conclusion, proper implementation and execution of a strategic plan are critical factors in achieving success. Companies that invest in effective execution by providing resources, training, and aligning departments can achieve great results. The ability to overcome execution challenges often leads to valuable lessons, ultimately building a more resilient and successful organization.

By the end of this chapter, you will have a comprehensive understanding of the critical role execution plays in achieving strategic goals. Effective implementation turns plans into reality, propelling your organization toward success, just as *diligent execution of a strategy brings about fruitful results.*

Chapter 10:

Measuring and Evaluating Strategy

In this final chapter, we will explore the essential processes of measuring and evaluating your strategic efforts. Effective assessment ensures that your strategy remains aligned with your goals and allows for adjustments based on results.

10.1 Key Performance Indicators (KPIs)

Much like the biblical principle of *"you will know them by their fruits"* **(Matthew 7:16, NIV),** in business, results matter. KPIs are the fruits of your strategic labor, and they provide valuable insights into your progress. We'll delve into:

- **What Are KPIs:** Defining KPIs and their role in measuring success.

- **Choosing Relevant KPIs:** Selecting the most meaningful metrics for your organization.

- **Setting Targets:** Establishing benchmarks and goals for KPIs.

- **Regular Monitoring:** The importance of ongoing KPI tracking.

10.2 Balanced Scorecard

The balanced scorecard is a strategic framework that looks beyond financial metrics to provide a more comprehensive view of organizational performance. We'll explore:

- **Four Perspectives of the Balanced Scorecard:** Financial, Customer, Internal Processes, and Learning and Growth.

- **Aligning Metrics:** How to align KPIs with each perspective.

- **Strategy Mapping:** Connecting strategic objectives with performance measures.

10.3 Adjusting Strategy Based on Results

The ability to adapt and adjust is essential for success, just as the Bible encourages us to be *"quick to listen" (James 1:19, NIV).* We'll discuss:

- **Continuous Improvement:** Cultivating a culture of continuous learning and adaptation.

- **Feedback Loops:** How to use KPI results and feedback to inform strategic decisions.

- **When to Pivot:** Recognizing when it's necessary to make significant changes to your strategy.

By the end of this chapter, you will have the tools and knowledge to effectively measure, evaluate, and adjust your strategic efforts. Just as in the parable of the talents *(Matthew 25:14-30, NIV),* effective measurement and evaluation enable you to steward your resources wisely, ensuring that your strategic investments yield the desired results and contribute to the long-term success of your organization.

Chapter 11:

Innovation and Adaptation

In this chapter, we will explore the dynamic concepts of innovation and adaptation within the realm of business strategy. These elements are essential for staying competitive and relevant in an ever-evolving market landscape.

11.1 The Role of Innovation in Strategy

Innovation is the engine of progress, propelling businesses forward and transforming industries. We'll delve into how innovation plays a pivotal role in shaping and executing successful business strategies:

- **Defining Innovation:** Understanding the various forms of innovation, from product and process innovation to business model innovation.

- **Fostering a Culture of Innovation:** Cultivating an environment that encourages creativity and the generation of new ideas.

- **Innovation as a Competitive Advantage:** How innovative products, services, or processes can set a business apart.

11.2 Adapting to Changing Markets

Change is a constant in the business world, much like the biblical principle that *"there is a time for everything"* **(Ecclesiastes 3:1, NIV).** Adapting to changing markets is a crucial element of effective strategy. We'll explore:

- **Market Dynamics:** How markets evolve and the impact of external factors.

- **Competitive Intelligence:** Strategies for staying informed about industry trends and competitor actions.

- **Flexibility and Resilience:** The importance of being agile and resilient in the face of change.

11.3 Case Studies of Adaptive Companies

Drawing inspiration from real-world examples can shed light on the power of innovation and adaptation. We'll explore case studies of companies that have successfully navigated change and embraced innovation:

- **Apple Inc.:** A case study on Apple's ability to continually innovate and adapt its product offerings.

- **Netflix:** How Netflix evolved from a DVD rental service to a global streaming giant.

- **Amazon:** A look at Amazon's expansion and diversification from an online bookstore to a tech and e-commerce behemoth.

These case studies will illustrate the strategies and tactics these companies employed to remain competitive and adaptive in their respective markets.

By the end of this chapter, you will appreciate the critical role that innovation and adaptation play in the success of a business strategy. Just as the biblical principle in ***Proverbs 24:5 (NIV)*** emphasizes the value of knowledge, innovative thinking and adaptability are forms of knowledge that empower organizations to thrive in an ever-changing world.

Chapter 12:

Managing Risk in Strategy

In this chapter, we will explore the vital aspect of managing risk within the context of business strategy. Identifying, mitigating, and effectively responding to risks is essential for ensuring the success and resilience of your strategic plans.

12.1 Identifying Business Risks

Just as in the biblical story of Noah, who took measures to prepare for the flood *(Genesis 6:14-16, NIV),* businesses must identify potential risks and prepare for them. We'll discuss:

- **Types of Business Risks:** Exploring various categories, including financial, operational, strategic, and external risks.

- **Risk Assessment:** Strategies for evaluating the likelihood and impact of identified risks.

- **Scenario Planning:** Preparing for various possible outcomes, particularly in uncertain environments.

12.2 Risk Mitigation Strategies

Risk management is like building a strong foundation; it ensures the stability and longevity of your strategic plans. We'll delve into strategies for mitigating and reducing risks:

- **Risk Avoidance:** Strategies for entirely avoiding high-risk activities or decisions.

- **Risk Reduction:** Measures to minimize the impact or likelihood of risks.

- **Risk Transfer:** Shifting risk to another party, such as through insurance or outsourcing.

- **Risk Acceptance:** Understanding and accepting certain risks when they align with strategic objectives.

12.3 Crisis Management

In life, as in business, crises can occur unexpectedly. How you respond to crises can define your organization's reputation and long-term success. We'll explore:

- **Crisis Preparedness:** The importance of having a well-defined crisis management plan.

- **Communication Strategies:** How to communicate effectively with stakeholders during a crisis.

- **Learning from Crises:** Extracting valuable lessons and making improvements based on crisis experiences.

By the end of this chapter, you will have a comprehensive understanding of the critical role that risk management plays in the success and sustainability of your business strategy. Just as the Bible offers guidance for navigating life's challenges, effective risk management ensures that your strategic plans can weather unforeseen storms and continue on the path to success.

Chapter 13:

International Business Strategy

In this chapter, we will explore the complexities and opportunities of international business strategy. Expanding globally requires a unique set of considerations and strategies to navigate diverse markets successfully.

13.1 Expanding Globally

Going global is akin to exploring uncharted territories, and it offers immense growth potential. We'll delve into the steps and considerations involved in expanding your business beyond domestic borders:

- **Motivations for International Expansion:** Exploring the reasons why businesses choose to go global, such as market growth, diversification, or resource access.

- **Market Selection:** How to identify and prioritize target international markets.

- **Legal and Regulatory Compliance:** Navigating the legal complexities of operating in foreign jurisdictions.

13.2 Cultural Considerations

Understanding and respecting cultural differences is paramount in international business, much like the biblical principle of *"love your neighbor as yourself" (Matthew 22:39, NIV).* We'll discuss:

- **Cultural Sensitivity:** The importance of being aware of and respecting local customs, values, and norms.

- **Cross-Cultural Communication:** Strategies for effective communication in multicultural settings.

- **Adaptation vs. Standardization:** Deciding whether to adapt products and services to local preferences or maintain a standardized global approach.

13.3 International Market Entry Strategies

Entering foreign markets requires careful planning and consideration of various strategies. We'll explore different approaches to international market entry:

- **Exporting:** Selling products or services to foreign markets from your home country.

- **Licensing and Franchising:** Granting rights to foreign entities to use your intellectual property or business model.

- **Joint Ventures and Alliances:** Partnering with local companies to enter a market.

- **Foreign Direct Investment (FDI):** Establishing a physical presence in a foreign market, such as subsidiaries or wholly-owned subsidiaries.

By the end of this chapter, you will have a comprehensive understanding of the intricacies and opportunities of international business strategy. Just as the Bible imparts wisdom about interacting with people from diverse backgrounds, international business strategy requires wisdom in navigating the complexities of global markets, cultures, and regulations.

Chapter 14:

Sustainable Business Strategies

In this chapter, we will explore the vital aspect of sustainability within the context of business strategy. Sustainable business practices encompass environmental and social responsibility and contribute to the triple bottom line—people, planet, and profit.

14.1 Sustainability in Business

Sustainability is akin to stewardship, a biblical principle that emphasizes responsible and ethical management of resources. We'll delve into the concept of sustainability in business:

- **Defining Sustainability:** Understanding what sustainability means in the business context, including environmental, social, and economic aspects.

- **Sustainable Development Goals (SDGs):** How businesses align with global sustainability objectives.

- **Benefits of Sustainability:** Exploring the advantages of integrating sustainability into business strategy, from improved reputation to cost savings.

14.2 Environmental and Social Responsibility

In business, as in life, responsibility extends beyond profit, echoing the biblical principle of loving one's neighbor. We'll discuss:

- **Environmental Responsibility:** Strategies for reducing environmental impact, such as energy efficiency, waste reduction, and sustainable sourcing.

- **Social Responsibility:** The importance of ethical practices, fair labor, and community engagement.

- **Corporate Social Responsibility (CSR):** How businesses can contribute to the betterment of society.

14.3 The Triple Bottom Line

The triple bottom line (TBL) is a framework that assesses an organization's performance based on three dimensions: people, planet, and profit. We'll explore how the TBL helps businesses evaluate their impact holistically:

- **People:** Considering the well-being and social impact on employees, customers, and communities.

- **Planet:** Assessing environmental impact, including resource consumption, emissions, and conservation efforts.

- **Profit:** Evaluating financial performance and profitability.

By the end of this chapter, you will have a comprehensive understanding of the significance of sustainable business strategies. Just as the Bible emphasizes responsibility toward others and stewardship of the Earth, sustainable business practices reflect a commitment to ethical, responsible, and environmentally conscious conduct in the pursuit of long-term success.

Chapter 15:

Case Studies

In this final chapter, we will explore real-world case studies of successful business strategies, drawing valuable lessons from these examples that can inspire and inform your own strategic endeavors.

15.1 Real-world Examples of Successful Business Strategies

We will delve into a diverse set of case studies that showcase businesses that have achieved remarkable success through strategic planning and execution. These case studies will encompass various industries and strategic approaches, illustrating the versatility and effectiveness of strategic thinking:

- **Apple Inc.:** An exploration of Apple's innovative product development and ecosystem-building strategies.

- **Google:** A look at how Google leveraged its search engine dominance to diversify and expand its services.

- **Tesla:** An examination of Tesla's disruptive approach to electric vehicles and renewable energy.

- **Walmart:** A case study on how Walmart's low-cost leadership strategy transformed the retail industry.

- **Airbnb:** An exploration of Airbnb's platform-based business model and its impact on the hospitality industry.

15.2 Lessons Learned

Each case study will be accompanied by a discussion of the key lessons and takeaways that can be applied to your own business strategy. We'll highlight the strategies, innovations, and best practices that contributed to the success of these organizations, providing you with valuable insights and inspiration.

By the end of this chapter, you will have gained a deeper understanding of effective business strategies through real-world examples. Just as the Bible contains parables and stories that impart wisdom, these case studies offer practical lessons that can inform and enhance your strategic thinking, helping you navigate the complexities of the business world with confidence and competence.

Chapter 16:

The Future of Business Strategy

In this closing chapter, we will gaze into the crystal ball of business strategy, exploring emerging trends, technologies, and the essential steps to prepare for the future in an ever-evolving business landscape.

16.1 Emerging Trends and Technologies

The future is akin to uncharted territory, filled with both challenges and opportunities. We'll delve into the emerging trends and technologies that are likely to shape the future of business strategy:

- **Digital Transformation:** How organizations are embracing digital technologies to optimize operations and customer experiences.

- **Artificial Intelligence (AI) and Automation:** The impact of AI and automation on decision-making, efficiency, and innovation.

- **Sustainability and ESG:** The growing importance of environmental, social, and governance (ESG) considerations in business strategy.

- **E-commerce and Omni-channel Retail:** The evolution of retail and consumer engagement in an online-dominated world.

- **Remote Work and Flexible Work Models:** The future of work and its implications for business strategy.

16.2 Preparing for the Future

Preparation is the key to navigating the uncertain future, much like the biblical principle of preparation and vigilance. We'll discuss the essential steps to prepare your business for what lies ahead:

- **Continuous Learning and Adaptation:** The importance of staying informed, fostering a culture of learning, and embracing change.

- **Innovation and Agility:** How to cultivate an innovative mindset and agile practices that allow for quick responses to emerging trends.

- **Scenario Planning:** Preparing for multiple possible futures and developing strategies to address each.

- **Talent and Leadership Development:** Nurturing the skills and capabilities needed for future success, and developing leadership that can guide your organization through change.

- **Sustainability and Responsible Practices:** Integrating sustainability and ethical considerations into your business strategy.

By the end of this chapter, you will have a glimpse of the potential future of business strategy and a roadmap for preparing your organization to thrive in an ever-changing environment. Just as the Bible imparts wisdom for facing the unknown, strategic preparation and adaptability are your compass and armor as you navigate the uncharted waters of the business world.

Conclusion:

Congratulations on completing this comprehensive journey through the world of business strategy! In this concluding chapter, we will recap the key concepts you've explored throughout this book and offer encouragement for applying the knowledge you've gained.

Recap of Key Concepts

In this book, we've covered a wide range of critical concepts in business strategy, including:

- The importance of strategy in business success.

- Different types of business strategies, from differentiation to cost leadership.

- Tools like SWOT analysis and market research for strategic decision-making.

- Setting goals, both short-term and long-term, and aligning them with your strategy.

- The strategic planning process and the creation of strategic plans.

- The significance of involving stakeholders in strategic planning.

- Strategies for turning your plans into actionable steps.

- Measuring and evaluating your strategic efforts through KPIs and the balanced scorecard.

- The role of innovation and adaptation in staying competitive.

- Managing risk and crisis effectively.

- Expanding globally and considering cultural factors.

- The importance of sustainability and corporate responsibility.

- Case studies of successful business strategies.

- Insights into emerging trends and technologies shaping the future of business strategy.

Encouragement to Apply What You've Learned

Knowledge is valuable when put into practice. As you reflect on the concepts presented in this book, we encourage you to take action. Apply what you've learned to your business endeavors, whether you're an aspiring entrepreneur, a seasoned executive, or anyone in between. Here's how:

- **Strategic Planning:** Take the time to craft a well-defined strategy for your business, aligning it with your vision and goals.

- **Continuous Learning:** Stay informed about emerging trends, technologies, and best practices in business strategy.

- **Innovation:** Foster a culture of innovation within your organization to remain competitive and adaptable.

- **Sustainability:** Consider the environmental and social impact of your business decisions and integrate sustainable practices.

- **Risk Management:** Identify potential risks and develop mitigation strategies to protect your business.

- **Global Expansion:** Explore opportunities for international growth while respecting local cultures and regulations.

- **Stakeholder Engagement:** Involve employees, customers, and partners in your strategic planning process.

- **Adaptation:** Be flexible and ready to adjust your strategy as market conditions evolve.

- **Measurement and Evaluation:** Implement KPIs and evaluation processes to monitor your progress toward strategic goals.

- **Responsibility:** Embrace corporate social responsibility and ethical practices in all aspects of your business.

As you apply these principles and strategies in your business journey, remember that success often involves perseverance, resilience, and a commitment to learning and improvement. Just as the Bible offers wisdom for living a fulfilling life, the principles of effective business strategy can guide you toward achieving your professional and organizational goals.

Thank you for embarking on this strategic voyage with us. We wish you every success in your future business endeavors, and may your strategies be guided by wisdom, ethics, and a vision for a brighter future.

Appendices:

In this section, you'll find valuable resources and tools to enhance your understanding of business strategy and assist you in applying what you've learned. These appendices include:

A. Additional Resources

Here, we provide a curated list of books, articles, websites, and courses that can deepen your knowledge of business strategy. Whether you're looking for more in-depth information on a specific topic or seeking to broaden your strategic horizons, these resources are a valuable reference.

B. Glossary of Key Terms

This glossary offers concise definitions of the key terms and concepts introduced throughout the book. It serves as a quick reference guide to help you navigate the terminology associated with business strategy.

C. Worksheets and Templates

Practical tools are essential for translating theory into action. In this section, you'll find worksheets, templates, and frameworks that can aid you in various aspects of strategic planning and execution. These resources include:

- **SWOT Analysis Template:** A structured template for conducting SWOT analyses.

- **SMART Goals Worksheet:** A tool to help you formulate specific, measurable, achievable, relevant, and time-bound goals.

- **Strategic Planning Template:** A framework for creating your strategic plan.

- **KPI Tracking Sheet:** A spreadsheet to track key performance indicators.

- **Scenario Planning Template:** A template for preparing for multiple possible futures.

- **Balanced Scorecard Template:** A framework for assessing performance from multiple perspectives.

These worksheets and templates are designed to simplify and streamline your strategic efforts, providing practical guidance for implementation.

With these appendices, we aim to provide you with the resources and tools you need to embark on your strategic journey with confidence and competence. Business strategy is not merely a theoretical concept; it's a practical and actionable discipline that can drive success in your professional endeavors. We wish you the best of luck as you continue to explore, learn, and apply the principles of business strategy.

Index:

- Comprehensive index for quick reference

www.ingramcontent.com/pod-product-compliance
Lightning Source LLC
Chambersburg PA
CBHW072052230526
45479CB00010B/797